COPYRIGHT

<u>Breakup to Breakthrough: a Follow-Up Guide: How to Turn a Breakup into a Breakthrough - Self - Care Coloring Workbook</u>
Copyright © 2023 of First Publication by Lesley D. Nurse
All rights reserved.
No portion of this book may be reproduced in any form without written permission from the publisher or author except as permitted by U.S. copyright law.
This publication is designed to provide accurate and authoritative information in regard to the subject matter covered. It is sold with the understanding that neither the author nor the publisher is engaged in rendering legal, investment, accounting, or other professional services. While the publisher and author have used their best efforts in preparing this book, they make no representations or warranties with respect to the accuracy or completeness of the contents of this book and specifically disclaim any implied warranties of merchantability or fitness for a particular purpose. No warranty may be created or extended by sales representatives or written sales materials. The advice and strategies contained herein may not be suitable for your situation. You should consult with a professional when appropriate. Neither the publisher nor the author shall be liable for any loss of profit or any other commercial damages, including but not limited to special, incidental, consequential, personal, or other damages.
Book Cover by Lesley D. Nurse
ISBN 979-8-218-24658-7

Disclaimer

These are the tips that have worked for me. If you feel that you might be experiencing challenges that require more significant help, please seek a medical professional.

Introduction

In my latest book, "How to Turn a Breakup into a Breakthrough," I wanted to delve deeper into the challenges and obstacles we face when trying to heal from a breakup. While we often hear the advice to move on and let go, there are times when the process feels overwhelming.

Introduction

That's why I have created "Breakup to Breakthrough: A Follow-Up Guide" self-care coloring workbook, filled with easy-to-follow ideas to help you relax and empower yourself on your healing journey. Remember, this is your journey, and you have complete control over it.

The Beauty of Healing from a Breakup

Healing from a breakup is like shedding a heavy weight off your shoulders, a warm hug from a caring friend, and basking in a sunny day's refreshing breeze. It's about reconnecting with the innocence of your inner child, experiencing unexpected personal growth, and opening yourself up to love and excitement.

The Beauty of Healing from a Breakup

Healing is a transformative breakthrough that lifts your spirits and brings a genuine smile to your face. And through this workbook, I invite you to have fun and embrace your journey with grace.

You are in complete control of designing your life. Color it joyfully & live it out bravely.

Embracing the Healing Process

When healing from a breakup, we often hear we should go on and let go of the past. But what if the process is not always pretty? Acknowledge challenges that come with healing. It's important to remember that healing is a personal journey, and you have complete control over it.

Recovering from the End of a Relationship: Coping with the Emotions

It's about reconnecting with the innocence of your inner child, experiencing unexpected personal growth, and opening yourself up to love and excitement. Transformative experiences can be the life-changing breakthrough that lifts your spirits and brings a genuine smile to your face.

Rediscovering the Joys of Freedom and Innocence.

Rediscovering one's unique identity through self-discovery can bring back the freedom of childhood and open up endless possibilities. Through this process, you'll experience unexpected personal growth, gaining wisdom and strength that will carry you forward.

Exploring New Love and Opportunities

Recovering from a breakup involves more than just releasing your attachment to the past. It also involves being receptive to new love and uncovering exciting new opportunities along the way. This workbook motivates you to welcome the concept of love once again and to have faith that there are amazing bonds waiting for you in the future. It's about embracing the unfamiliar and being willing to explore the possibilities that await you.

Embrace Your Healing Journey: Transforming Pain into Power.

Recovering from a breakup is a transformative process that enables you to turn pain into power ultimately. It requires finding that breakthrough moment that lifts your spirits and brings a genuine smile to your face. Through this workbook, I invite you to gracefully embrace your recovery journey, which is unique to you. It will give you the strength to overcome any obstacle that comes your way.

Seize control of your life and enhance it at every opportunity. Embrace your independence and strengthen yourself.

Don't let limiting beliefs hold you back. Embrace freedom, pursue your desires, and move forward with confidence. Nothing should stop you from achieving your goals.

Achieving Resilience and Triumph

Through persistence and determination, we must confront challenges in order to grow and develop as individuals. This not only increases our resilience but also equips us with the necessary tools to tackle future obstacles with confidence.

Mastering the Art of Embracing Silence and Letting Go of Worries.

To enhance your resilience during challenging times, it's best to concentrate on identifying solutions instead of fixating on the issues themselves. Additionally, allocating some time to achieve inner peace and tranquility can aid in fostering a more optimistic mindset.

Never reveal a hint of sweat. Stay cool, calm, and collected in all situations.

Lesley

Be prepared to walk away if you assert being strong enough to do so.

Lesley

Don't try to make others see your value, as it may result in them seeing less of it.

Lesley

Embracing New Beginnings: Finding Strength in the Aftermath of a Breakup

The aftermath of a breakup can be a journey of self-discovery, where you uncover newfound strength within yourself and decide to halt the pain and move forward. Whether it's a continuous or a moment of realization, dealing with a breakup can lead to personal growth and embracing new beginnings.

The Journey to True Happiness: Unveiling Mental and Growth in Outer Relationships and in Time

Discovering true happiness is a voyage of relationships and fleeting moments in our lives. During these times, we open new doors to our mental and spiritual realms, paving the way for personal growth and progress toward true happiness.

Don't hesitate to release. Simply take action.

In order to achieve optimal health and mental clarity, it is crucial to release any negative emotions from past struggles and hardships. By resetting your thoughts and gaining a fresh outlook, you can unlock greater opportunities for personal growth and happiness in your life.

Mastering Life and Love After a Breakup

After a breakup, it's important to avoid distractions and take time for self-discovery. Don't settle for less than a great match. Believe in finding a fulfilling, honest relationship that helps you grow.

TO WITNESS WHAT IS POSSIBLE, HAVE FAITH IN THE POWER OF BELIEF.

When healing from a breakup, focus on something that brings you joy. Reprogram your thoughts with positivity by picturing something happy and repeating a positive affirmation. A positive attitude, gratitude, and self-assurance can bring endless opportunities.

I hope that now you feel more optimistic and inspired by acknowledging how much progress you've made simply by choosing to do so. It's understandable if you're not feeling your best, but it's okay. By concentrating on what you can control and what could be, rather than dwelling on the past and what you're accustomed to, you open yourself up to a new perspective with limitless potential.

Your breakthrough starts now...

Unblock Your Joy

Having clear objectives can lead to unexpected achievements. It's crucial to ensure your goals align with your deepest desires, and you're free to have as many objectives as you want.

GOAL	TO DO LIST

This exercise is an effective way to advance your skills and promote healing, all while avoiding self-criticism.

BREAKTHROUGH

Daily Journal

DATES :   **MOOD :**

Before I dated them, I was...

_____

_____

_____

_____

_____

_____

BEFORE I DATED THEM, I WAS...

BEFORE I DATED THEM, I WAS...

BEFORE I DATED THEM, I WAS...

BEFORE I DATED THEM, I WAS...

BEFORE I DATED THEM, I WAS...

This exercise is an effective way to advance your skills and promote healing, all while avoiding self-criticism.

BREAKTHROUGH

Daily Journal

DATES : **MOOD :**

While I dated them, I was...

....

....

....

....

....

....

WHILE I DATED THEM, I WAS...

WHILE I DATED THEM, I WAS...

WHILE I DATED THEM, I WAS...

WHILE I DATED THEM, I WAS...

WHILE I DATED THEM, I WAS...

THIS EXERCISE IS AN EFFECTIVE WAY TO ADVANCE YOUR SKILLS AND PROMOTE HEALING, ALL WHILE AVOIDING SELF-CRITICISM.

BREAKTHROUGH

Daily Journal

DATES :   **MOOD :**

AFTER I DATED THEM, I WAS...

....

....

....

....

....

....

AFTER I DATED THEM, I WAS...

AFTER I DATED THEM, I WAS...

AFTER I DATED THEM, I WAS...

AFTER I DATED THEM, I WAS...

AFTER I DATED THEM, I WAS...

Unblock Your Joy

Having clear objectives can lead to unexpected achievements. It's crucial to ensure your goals align with your deepest desires, and you're free to have as many objectives as you want.

GOAL

TO DO LIST

This exercise is an effective way to advance your skills and promote healing, all while avoiding self-criticism.

BREAKTHROUGH

Daily Journal

DATES :   **MOOD :**

Before I dated them, I was...

....

....

....

....

....

....

....

BEFORE I DATED THEM, I WAS...

BEFORE I DATED THEM, I WAS...

BEFORE I DATED THEM, I WAS...

BEFORE I DATED THEM, I WAS...

BEFORE I DATED THEM, I WAS...

This exercise is an effective way to advance your skills and promote healing, all while avoiding self-criticism.

BREAKTHROUGH

Daily Journal

DATES :   MOOD :

WHILE I DATED THEM, I WAS...

....

....

....

....

....

....

....

WHILE I DATED THEM, I WAS...

WHILE I DATED THEM, I WAS...

WHILE I DATED THEM, I WAS...

WHILE I DATED THEM, I WAS...

WHILE I DATED THEM, I WAS...

This exercise is an effective way to advance your skills and promote healing, all while avoiding self-criticism.

BREAKTHROUGH

Daily Journal

DATES : **MOOD :**

After I dated them, I was...

....

....

....

....

....

....

....

AFTER I DATED THEM, I WAS...

AFTER I DATED THEM, I WAS...

AFTER I DATED THEM, I WAS...

AFTER I DATED THEM, I WAS...

AFTER I DATED THEM, I WAS...

This exercise is an effective way to advance your skills and promote healing, all while avoiding self-criticism.

BREAKTHROUGH

Daily Journal

DATES : **MOOD :**

BEFORE I DATED THEM, I WAS...

....

....

....

....

....

....

....

BEFORE I DATED THEM, I WAS...

BEFORE I DATED THEM, I WAS...

BEFORE I DATED THEM, I WAS...

BEFORE I DATED THEM, I WAS...

BEFORE I DATED THEM, I WAS...

This exercise is an effective way to advance your skills and promote healing, all while avoiding self-criticism.

BREAKTHROUGH

Daily Journal

DATES :   **MOOD :**

While I Dated Them, I Was...

....

....

....

....

....

....

WHILE I DATED THEM, I WAS...

WHILE I DATED THEM, I WAS...

WHILE I DATED THEM, I WAS...

WHILE I DATED THEM, I WAS...

WHILE I DATED THEM, I WAS...

This exercise is an effective way to advance your skills and promote healing, all while avoiding self-criticism.

BREAKTHROUGH

Daily Journal

DATES :   **MOOD :**

AFTER I DATED THEM, I WAS...

_____

_____

_____

_____

_____

_____

_____

AFTER I DATED THEM, I WAS...

AFTER I DATED THEM, I WAS...

AFTER I DATED THEM, I WAS...

AFTER I DATED THEM, I WAS...

AFTER I DATED THEM, I WAS...

This exercise is an effective way to advance your skills and promote healing, all while avoiding self-criticism.

BREAKTHROUGH

Daily Journal

DATES : **MOOD :**

Today, I am...

....

....

....

....

....

....

....

TODAY, I AM...

TODAY, I AM...

TODAY, I AM...

TODAY, I AM...

TODAY, I AM...

Sometimes, a relationship doesn't end romantically. It could be cutting ties with friends, family, a business, a job, or something else. It's important to remember that this is your journey, and if it's causing you to lose peace or threaten your happiness, you have the power to say "Enough is enough" and move forward.

Daily Journal

DATES :   MOOD :

Enough is enough and I am ...

....
....
....
....
....
....
....

Enough is enough and I am ...

Enough is enough and I am ...

Enough is enough and I am ...

Enough is enough and I am ...

Enough is enough and I am ...

Greetings on the start of your new journey, where you take center stage in your own life. Treat yourself with kindness and let go of the past as you embark on this path. Seize the moment and all the opportunities it presents. This journey will help you find a partner and discover your true self while also providing insights into how others will perceive you in the future. Recognize your worth and remember that you are enough.
Wishing you all the best on your incredible journey ahead!
With love
and light, Lesley.

LESLEY D. NURSE

WWW.LESLEYNURSE.COM

Break Free and Create Your Dream Life

Lesley is a dynamic force dedicated to empowering individuals to break free from the shackles of their own limitations and unlock their true potential. With a burning passion for helping others, Lesley has made it her life's mission for people to create the life they desire.

With her captivating books and numerous other pursuits, Lesley invites you to embark on a transformative journey of self-discovery and personal growth. Her words resonate with authenticity, wisdom, and a deep understanding of the human experience.

Visit Lesley's website to explore her captivating collection of books and delve into her diverse range of passions. Get inspired to embrace change, unlock your potential, and manifest the life you've always dreamed of. Lesley's unwavering commitment to your empowerment ensures a trustworthy and engaging experience that will leave you feeling motivated and ready to conquer what comes your way.

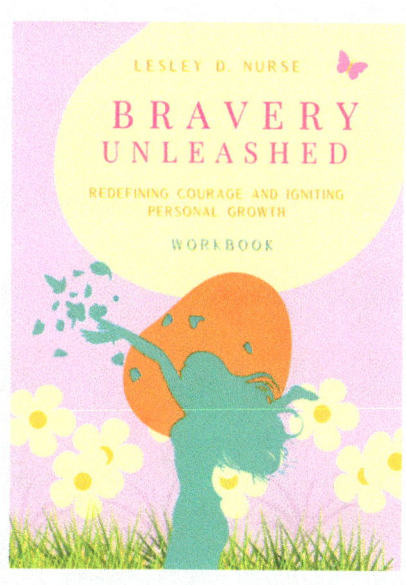

During a breakup, it's imperative that you remain resilient and hold onto your self-worth. For an instant confidence boost, check out my workbook, Bravery Unleashed: Redefining Courage and Igniting Personal Growth. This guide is specially designed to help you explore your true self in a secure and supportive environment, let go of negative thought patterns, and unleash your hidden bravery. Remember, life can be tough, but with the help of this workbook, you'll be back on track in no time.

INFO@7SEVENSPARKPUBLISHING.COM

WWW.7SEVENSPARKPUBLISHING.COM

www.ingramcontent.com/pod-product-compliance
Lightning Source LLC
Chambersburg PA
CBHW080550030426
42337CB00024B/4824